Faith Connections

Bible Study Guide
Large Print

Summer
23

Holy Living

Hard Sayings of the Old Testament

Titus and Philemon

Bible Study Guide

Contents

Summer 2023
Volume 46, Number 4

Adult Bible Study Guide is one of several Faith Connections companion products, a themed suite of resources designed to help adults discover what it means to be holy people in today's world. To order, call 1-800-877-0700.

Mike L. Wonch
Editor

Cover Photo: © Don Pablo/Shutterstock.com

All scripture quotations, unless otherwise indicated, are taken from the *Holy Bible, New International Version* (NIV). Copyright © 1973, 1978, 1984, 2011 by Biblica Inc. Used by permission. All rights reserved.

All Scripture quotations marked † are the author's own translation from the original languages.

The following copyrighted versions are used by permission:

From the *New Revised Standard Version* (NRSV) of the Bible, copyright 1989 by the Division of Christian Education of the National Council of the Churches of Christ in the USA. Used by permission. All rights reserved.

We believe in the full inspiration of the Scripture and encourage the comparison and use of several translations as part of the discipline of Bible study.

Bible Study Guide is published quarterly by The Foundry Publishing®, P.O. Box 419527, Kansas City, MO 64141. Copyright © 2023 by The Foundry Publishing®. Canadian GST No. R129017471.

Perspectives

Keep Moving Forward

Once in a while I will get the urge to look through old photo albums, which includes my baby book and a scrapbook from my teen years. It is fun to see all the places I have been, the people I have known, and the things I have done. As I thumb through the pages, however, I never think, "Oh, I wish I were a baby again" or "If only I was 14 again." I look at the past with fond memories, seeing the good and bad that has happened at each stage of life, which has led me to where I am today. Yet, I realize that I am not meant to live in the past, only thinking about the "good old days." Life is to be lived forward.

When I look back on my spiritual journey, I have many great memories. I think back to youth camps, revivals, mission trips, and so on that have had a spiritual impact on of my life. These were special times when God was working and moving in my life. Although I am thankful for these moments in time, I never long for, spiritually speaking, the "good old days." My spiritual life must be lived forward.

There is a benefit to looking back. We can appreciate moments when we felt God's presence especially near or times when He worked in a special way in and/or through our lives. We can look back in thankfulness for God's faithfulness and transforming power. However, we cannot live in the spiritual past. God calls us, regardless of age or spiritual maturity, to keep moving forward on our spiritual journey, growing each day. Psalm 92:12-14 says, "The righteous will flourish like a palm tree, they will grow like a cedar of Lebanon; planted in the house of the LORD, they will flourish in the courts of our God. They will still bear fruit in old age, they will stay fresh and green."

During this quarter, take time to look back at special moments in your spiritual life, thanking God for those times. But don't stop there. Look forward, asking God to lead you in the ways that help you continually grow in your faith and draw closer to Him each day.

May God bless you as you study His Word this quarter!

MIKE WONCH
Editor

June

4

CHRISTLIKE ATTITUDES

Christlikeness means reflecting the attitude of Christ.

THE WORD

ECCLESIASTES 7:1-14

A good name is better than fine perfume, and the day of death better than the day of birth.

²It is better to go to a house of mourning than to go to a house of feasting, for death is the destiny of everyone; the living should take this to heart.

³Frustration is better than laughter, because a sad face is good for the heart.

⁴The heart of the wise is in the house of mourning, but the heart of fools is in the house of pleasure.

⁵It is better to heed the rebuke of a wise person than to listen to the song of fools.

⁶Like the crackling of thorns under the pot, so is the laughter of fools. This too is meaningless.

⁷Extortion turns a wise person into a fool, and a bribe corrupts the heart.

⁸The end of a matter is better than its beginning, and patience is better than pride.

⁹Do not be quickly provoked in your spirit, for anger resides in the lap of fools.

¹⁰Do not say, "Why were the old days better than these?" For it is not wise to ask such questions.

¹¹Wisdom, like an inheritance, is a good thing and benefits those who see the sun.

¹²Wisdom is a shelter as money is a shelter,
but the advantage of knowledge is this: Wisdom preserves those who have it.

¹³Consider what God has done: Who can straighten what he has made crooked?

¹⁴When times are good, be happy; but when times are bad, consider this: God has made the one as well as the other.
Therefore, no one can discover anything about their future.

ROMANS 12:1-2

KEY VERSE

¹Therefore, I urge you, brothers and sisters, in view of God's mercy, to offer your bodies as a living sacrifice, holy and pleasing to God—this is your true and proper worship. **²Do not conform to the pattern of this world, but be transformed by the renewing of your mind. Then you will be able to test and approve what God's will is—his good, pleasing and perfect will.**

ENGAGE THE WORD

WISDOM IN PERSPECTIVE

Ecclesiastes 7:1-10

Wisdom plays an important role in life; however, even wisdom itself must be kept within perspective. It has limitations. Verse 1 reminds us that a good name has value, but it cannot be the driving force of life. Verse 2 emphasizes the importance of living our days with an awareness of our mortality. As much as we might prefer to avoid it, suffering can teach important life lessons that we may never discover during good times, says verse 3.

Throughout this passage of Scripture, we are reminded of keeping good experiences, bad experiences, excitement, discouragement, accomplishments, and disappointments of life in perspective. A wise person discerns and understands the importance of perspective. However, verse 7 cautions that even human wisdom has its limits. Extortion or a bribe can cause even a wise person to falter in life.

Wise people know how to choose between patience, pride, provocations, and anger. They choose godly responses over carnal ones. The reference to the good old days in verse 10 refers back to the unwise attitude of the Hebrew people escaping through the desert following their liberation from Egyptian captivity. Even though Moses was leading them to God's promised

GOD RULES OVER ALL

land, they longed to go back to their familiar lives in Egypt (Exodus 16:3).

This passage focuses attention on the important reminder that throughout our Christian lives we make daily choices that are influenced by our attitudes. The inherent limitation of human wisdom reminds us that we do not have perfect perspective or judgment.

Ecclesiastes 7:11-14

Even with its limits, human wisdom has value. It offers an advantage to making the most of life, much like an inheritance from family or loved ones. Nevertheless, truly wise people admit needing something more to make the most of life. Rather, they need Someone, that is, they need a relationship with God in order to keep human life on this earth in proper perspective. We do not have perfect perspective or judgment. Therefore, we need to rely totally and completely on God for His will and leading for our lives.

Verse 13 reminds us that our God is sovereign over all creation. He establishes the framework of our universe and rules over it supremely. All of the human wisdom of the ages can never equal the almighty wisdom and power of God. Therefore, we should enjoy the good times in life and learn valuable lessons from the hard times all with a mindset that God rules supremely over everything in creation and in our lives.

GOD'S WILL IN OUR LIVES

Romans 12:1-2

The material in Ecclesiastes sets the stage for Paul's practical application in Romans 12. Believers who live in daily relationship with Jesus Christ develop the mind of Christ over time (1 Corinthians 2:16). This Christlike way of thinking and living affects more than right belief and righteous conduct; it also influences the very attitudes that work in the background of our lives.

Paul encourages us to offer the new life we have in Christ back to Him as a part of our gratitude and worship for all He has done in our lives. Worshipers offered animal sacrifices on the altars of the tabernacle and temple in the Old Testament. New Testament believers recognize that Jesus offered the ultimate and final sacrifice for our sins on the cross when He died in our place. Jesus did not just take our place on the cross; He offers us an example for the way we should think and live sacrificially. Therefore, we now identify with Him by having the same self-sacrificing attitude as He had. Unlike the animal sacrifices, we remain alive and work as the hands and feet of Jesus in our world.

Here are Christlike attitudes that should flavor our thinking and living.

1. *A hunger to know more.* A Christlike believer studies the Bible, prays, worships, participates in the sacraments, spends time with other Christians along with a host of other Christian disciplines.

2. *A discernment of application.* A Christlike believer grows in wisdom in order to apply everything the Spirit of God teaches us for daily living.

3. *A rejection of folly.* A Christlike believer judges the foolish ways of thinking and living by those who do not know Christ and choose to reject His path.

4. *A humble spirit.* A Christlike believer realizes that the knowledge and wisdom that can be known this side of eternity is limited and incomplete and humbly admits this.

5. *A worshipful awareness.* A Christlike believer testifies to the sovereignty of God in all of our lives and in all of creation.

6. *A transformed mindset.* A Christlike believer lives in the daily awareness that the Spirit of God living within is constantly working to transform us into the image of God's Son.

Think About It

We rub shoulders with many people every day who choose to live with skeptical, critical, hateful, or negative attitudes that color the way they view their world and everyone in it. If we are not mindful, we can be influenced by their perspective. We must allow the Holy Spirit to perfect Christlike attitudes in us as we consecrate ourselves fully to Him.

REFLECT Take time this week to allow God to do an attitude check in your life.

FRANK MOORE is retired general editor for the Church of the Nazarene.

June

11

CHRISTLIKE ENTERTAINMENT

Christlike living embraces the goodness of God in our world.

THE WORD

PSALM 101:1-8

I will sing of your love and justice; to you, LORD, I will sing praise. ²I will be careful to lead a blameless life—when will you come to me? I will conduct the affairs of my house with a blameless heart.

³I will not look with approval on anything that is vile. I hate what faithless people do; I will have no part in it.

⁴The perverse of heart shall be far from me; I will have nothing to do with what is evil.

⁵Whoever slanders their neighbor in secret, I will put to silence; whoever has haughty eyes and a proud heart, I will not tolerate.

⁶My eyes will be on the faithful in the land, that they may dwell with me; the one whose walk is blameless will minister to me.

⁷No one who practices deceit will dwell in my house; no one who speaks falsely will stand in my presence.

⁸Every morning I will put to silence all the wicked in the land; I will cut off every evildoer from the city of the LORD.

PHILIPPIANS 4:8-9

KEY VERSE

⁸Finally, brothers and sisters, whatever is true, whatever is noble, whatever is right, whatever is pure, whatever is lovely, whatever is admirable—if anything is excellent or praiseworthy—think about such things. ⁹Whatever you have learned or received or heard from me, or seen in me—put it into practice. And the God of peace will be with you.

ENGAGE THE WORD

VIRTUES TO UPHOLD

Psalm 101:1-2, 6

The psalmist begins Psalm 101 with some of the virtues he plans to uphold as the leader of God's people. He prefaces these highlighted virtues with the reminder that they originate in the love and justice of God. So, he praises and worships our God who rules the world with love and justice. He commits to living a blameless life. We must not confuse blamelessness with faultlessness. The psalmist's conduct may not be perfect in every way, but it can be free from sinful desires, motives, or intentions. He realizes that he can only live blamelessly as he depends on God (i.e., "When will you come to me?", v. 2). Everyone in the palace and in his home will witness his integrity of heart. The psalmist reminds us today that people in our homes, at school, and at work are watching our lives. Like the psalmist, we can only live blameless lives as we depend on God.

The psalmist commits to focus special attention on those who determine to live blameless lives before God and others just as he does. These individuals will hold him accountable to his commitment as they journey through life together. The integrity, honesty, and goodness that flows from their lives will encourage the psalmist in his pursuit of righteous living and together their examples will bless the entire nation.

INFLUENCES TO AVOID

Psalm 101:3-5, 7-8

The psalmist vows to disapprove of all that is vile or wicked. He will hate and not participate in the lifestyle choices of those who rebel against God's law and plan for our lives. The reference to the perverse of heart in verse 4 means both the twisted behavior as well as the deep longing within for such behavior. It is the opposite of a blameless heart and lifestyle (v. 2). The psalmist will not participate in thought or action with such twisted behavior. Furthermore, he vows to oppose those who lie or have attitudes of pride and arrogance.

VALUES TO LIVE BY

Not only will the psalmist refuse to participate in the deceit and lies of those within his community, he will not tolerate falsehood within his own household. He vows to promote biblical morality both at home and throughout the kingdom over which he rules. The psalmist reminds us today that the promotion of biblical justice, righteousness, and integrity within any nation requires good examples from top leaders. He also calls us to avoid giving attention to or participating in all lifestyle choices that rebel against God's laws and plan for our lives.

Philippians 4:8-9

Paul borrowed the list of values found in this passage of Scripture from the Greek and Roman culture of his day. Hence, these values are good for both those within the household of faith and everyone in society. Paul's cultural adaptation of these values reminds us that many of the virtues of our faith are highly regarded by those who have yet to come to faith. However, Paul knows that no one can live up to these lofty goals without the power of the Holy Spirit working within us making us Christlike. We must have the mind of Christ (Philippians 2:5) in order to live the virtues to which culture and our Christian faith call us.

Paul urges us to think about (or be entertained by) that which promotes what is true (real), noble (awe-inspiring), right (righteous as defined by God), pure (ethically holy), lovely (beautiful and attractive to others), and admirable (winsome). Together, these values call us to think about and be entertained by that which promotes moral excellence and praise from both God and those with whom we live and work. Paul knows we cannot perfect these values in our lives through human striving. We must live with the mind of Christ and in the power of the Holy Spirit. This call to virtuous living flows from the gospel of Christ, which transforms us into new creatures in Christ who live godly lives in our sin-filled world (2 Corinthians 5:17).

Think About It

The entertainment choices we make are seldom morally neutral. They carry a message that either resonates with the Christian faith or opposes it. This affects our thinking in ways that either draw us closer to our Lord Jesus Christ or hinder the all-important relationship we have with Him on a daily basis.

Verse 9 reminds us that Paul does not call us to these godly values without offering an example to follow. He invites his readers to follow his example as he, in turn, follows Christ's example (Philippians 2:6-11). Christ not only called His disciples to high moral standards, but He also modeled those standards in everyday living.

Paul ended this exhortation with a promise. That is, if you think in these ways and make wise choices that promote them, "the God of peace will be with you" (v. 9). Peace of heart and mind are in short supply in our world. This passage of Scripture has the answer: God, both the source and the giver of peace.

The two passages of Scripture in today's study offer important guidelines for making entertainment choices that honor Christ and make us more like Him.

1. Before making an entertainment choice, we should prayerfully submit to the Holy Spirit's leading.

2. We must choose wisely because people are watching our entertainment choices.

3. We should spend time with friends who can hold us accountable for our choices.

4. We should avoid entertainment that rebels against God's law and plan for our lives and promotes godless behavior.

5. We must depend upon God to give us the mind of Christ and the power of the Holy Spirit to make wise entertainment choices.

6. Always keep in mind that the entertainment choices we make affects the way we think, which in turn affects the things we value and the way we live.

REFLECT Take time this week to evaluate your entertainment choices in light of today's Scripture passages.

FRANK MOORE

June

18

CHRISTLIKE VIEW OF MONEY AND POSSESSIONS

The accumulation of wealth and material possessions is not the final goal in life.

THE WORD

ECCLESIASTES 5:10-20

Whoever loves money never has enough; whoever loves wealth is never satisfied with their income. This too is meaningless.

¹¹As goods increase, so do those who consume them. And what benefit are they to the owners except to feast their eyes on them?

¹²The sleep of a laborer is sweet, whether they eat little or much, but as for the rich, their abundance permits them no sleep.

¹³I have seen a grievous evil under the sun: wealth hoarded to the harm of its owners,

¹⁴or wealth lost through some misfortune, so that when they have children there is nothing left for them to inherit.

¹⁵Everyone comes naked from their mother's womb, and as everyone comes, so they depart. They take nothing from their toil that they can carry in their hands.

¹⁶This too is a grievous evil: As everyone comes, so they depart, and what do they gain, since they toil for the wind?

¹⁷All their days they eat in darkness, with great frustration, affliction and anger.

¹⁸This is what I have observed to be good: that it is appropriate for a person to eat, to drink and to find satisfaction in their toilsome labor under the sun during the few days of life God has given them—for this is their lot. ¹⁹Moreover, when God gives someone wealth and possessions, and the ability to enjoy them, to accept their lot and be happy in their toil—this is a gift of God. ²⁰They seldom reflect on the days of their life, because God keeps them occupied with gladness of heart.

MATTHEW 6:19-21

KEY VERSE

¹⁹"Do not store up for yourselves treasures on earth, where moths and vermin destroy, and where thieves break in and steal. ²⁰But store up for yourselves treasures in heaven, where moths and vermin do not destroy, and where thieves do not break in and steal. ²¹**For where your treasure is, there your heart will be also.**

ENGAGE THE WORD

THE BROKEN PROMISE OF RICHES

Ecclesiastes 5:10-17

For as long as currency has existed people have had to choose how they would value it and whether they would seek after it or not. This passage of Scripture warns against listening to the promise of riches.

Riches promise satisfaction in life with the accumulation of money and wealth. However, people from every generation in every culture seeking satisfaction in life through riches have testified that it does not truly satisfy. The accumulation of money and wealth create an addiction that can never be satisfied. The more you have the more you want.

Riches promise meaning in life. It seldom adds meaning to life. Rather, the more one drinks from its well the thirstier one gets. It fosters a love that becomes all-consuming yet never satisfying. Therefore, the affection for riches is meaningless.

Riches promise a solution to all of life's problems. Those who chase after it claim that they do not have any problem that more money would not solve. Yet, those who amass great fortunes claim that they have more problems than ever and problems associated with their wealth keep them up at night.

Riches promise permanent status in life. It promises a great reputation in future generations by passing wealth down to children and grandchildren. Yet, fortunes can be lost through a change in circumstances and the next generation inherits nothing. Riches cannot profit us in death. We come into the world with nothing, and we leave with nothing. After working the daylight hours of life amassing wealth, those chasing

THE BLESSING OF GODLY CONTENTMENT

riches go into darkness with great frustration, affliction, and anger. How sad!

Ecclesiastes 5:18-20

The God who created our world, everything in it, including humanity, directs us plainly on this subject. First, God wants us to be satisfied with what we have. Money and the possessions they buy can add meaning to our lives if we adopt an attitude of satisfaction with what God had entrusted into our hands.

Next, we must also remember that our days on this earth are limited; so, we must enjoy every day we have to work and our time with friends and family members. We must resist the temptation to fall into the addiction of seeking more of everything material.

Third, we must live with the awareness that the money and possessions we have are gifts from God. Who better to receive a gift from than our Creator? How better to thank Him for that gift than to live with the satisfaction that He is our provider. That attitude keeps money and possessions in their proper perspective.

Fourth, we find contentment in coming to terms with the fact that we are not ultimately in control of our lives. We willingly surrender that control to our sovereign God who always has our best interest in mind. Those who live with the mistaken impressing that they are in control of their lives are often shocked back to reality with their inability to control the doctor's grim medical diagnosis or a catastrophic collapse of the stock market. Health and fortune can evaporate in a day. Those resting calmly in God's sovereign hand trust themselves into His care.

Finally, and best of all, those who live with godly contentment find themselves consumed with the gladness of heart that only God can give. Words cannot express the value or worth in God's gift of heart gladness. It offers a foretaste of what is to come when we live with Him in eternity. We must never take God's

14

Think About It

Material wealth is a gift from God. Many people make this gift their god. Money and the possessions it can purchase become all-consuming idols that blind them to their need for God.

THE TREASURES IN HEAVEN

peace and gladness for granted. What an incredible gift!

Matthew 6:19-21

Jesus knew the Scriptures well and echoes the truth from Ecclesiastes 5:10-20 in the Sermon on the Mount. Jesus introduced an important perspective on the subject, however. Ecclesiastes 5 considers the proper place of money and possessions while living on earth. Jesus challenges us in this passage to consider life on earth from an eternal perspective.

Money and possessions have limited value when compared to the economy of heaven. Believers must live with an eternal perspective. Jesus is not condemning money or personal possessions. The notion of treasuring something gives it a central place in the owner's heart. A treasure is not simply currency or possession; it is highly valued by the owner. It supposedly earns status, security, or pride for the owner. In reality, however, it can lead the owner into materialism, consumerism, or preoccupation with earthly values.

Jesus redefines the commonly held notion of treasure. True treasure cannot be stored as currency or prized possessions. If it can rot, be bought, sold, destroyed, or stolen, it is not eternal treasure. Rather, true treasure reaches beyond earthly things to heavenly ones. The very definition of heaven draws us into the presence of God: Father, Son, and Holy Spirit. Jesus indicates that the heart of the matter is a matter of the heart. In other words, the values we hold near and dear on earth place our treasure either in this life or the eternal one.

REFLECT Consider that what we treasure most reveals the true allegiance of our hearts and the destiny of our souls.

FRANK MOORE

June

25

CHRISTLIKE DIALOGUE

*When encountering an opposing viewpoint,
our conversation should reflect a Christlike spirit.*

THE WORD

**PROVERBS
10:11-14**

The mouth of the righteous is a fountain of life, but the mouth of the wicked conceals violence.

¹²Hatred stirs up conflict, but love covers over all wrongs.

¹³Wisdom is found on the lips of the discerning, but a rod is for the back of one who has no sense.

¹⁴The wise store up knowledge, but the mouth of a fool invites ruin.

18-21

¹⁸Whoever conceals hatred with lying lips and spreads slander is a fool.

¹⁹Sin is not ended by multiplying words, but the prudent hold their tongues.

²⁰The tongue of the righteous is choice silver but the heart of the wicked is of little value.

²¹The lips of the righteous nourish many, but fools die for lack of sense.

31-32

³¹From the mouth of the righteous comes the fruit of wisdom, but a perverse tongue will be silenced.

³²The lips of the righteous know what finds favor, but the mouth of the wicked only what is perverse.

**PROVERBS
15:1-4**

¹A gentle answer turns away wrath, but a harsh word stirs up anger.

²The tongue of the wise adorns knowledge, but the mouth of the fool gushes folly.

³The eyes of the Lᴏʀᴅ are everywhere, keeping watch on the wicked and the good.

KEY VERSE ⁴**The soothing tongue is a tree of life, but a perverse tongue crushes the spirit.**

ENGAGE THE WORD

WORDS HAVE POWER

Proverbs 10:11-14

Proverbs 10 remind us that the words of a righteous person have the power to offer a fountain of life to others. These words can lift people's spirits and give them important insights for living a life pleasing to God. The words of a righteous person flow from a heart of love. This supernatural love originates in the heart of God who shares divine love with His children. They, in turn, serve as channels for God to reach out to others with His love.

The words of an unrighteous person also have power; their words promote violence, distrust, disrespect, and disharmony in the lives of others. Their words stir the pot that leads to conflict between their hearers. This conflict has the power to create division within families, communities, and entire nations. This power draws its strength from hatred in the human heart. Such hatred causes people to act in destructive ways as Satan leads people away from the blessings of life that only the Lord can give. God's love described in the previous paragraph has the power to overcome all of the hatred and wrongs created by the conversations of the unrighteous.

The language of the righteous is filled with wisdom. It offers important insights for abundant living. The righteous guard their God-given wisdom like a treasure and share it so others may know God's guidance for meaningful living. Not so with the language of the unrighteous. It offers nothing worth hearing and causes listeners to rebuke those who speak in such ways. Their foolish words are worthless and lead to ruin. In short, this passage of Scripture highlights the important reminder that

WORDS ARE A WINDOW

WORDS BRING RESULTS

we choose conversations that either bless others or harm them.

Proverbs 10:18-21, 31-32

During His earthly ministry, Jesus reminded us that the words we speak and the choices we make in life are a window into our soul. Matthew 23:25-29 teaches that people can use words and act in ways that appear to be righteous, but when examined more carefully reveal a heart filled with greed, self-righteousness, hypocrisy, and wickedness. Jesus said we must clean up our attitudes, motives, intentions, and desires. Then, righteous words and actions will flow from a purified heart.

This passage of Scripture in Proverbs also teaches that the words we speak and the choices we make in life are a window into our soul. A heart filled with hatred leads to lies, gossip, and slander. Such sinful people attempt to make their case or prove their point by talking on and on. However, a multitude of false words never add up to truth. Their words betray the reality that their heart contains nothing of value.

In contrast, a heart filled with God's presence and love leads to a few carefully chosen words that are of great value. The righteous speak honestly and to the point. They hold back from exaggeration or filling the air with meaningless words. Their Christlike conversation is valued like silver because people enjoy listening to what they have to say. They provide godly insight into the best ways of living. Their conversation nourishes people's hearts and minds.

Proverbs 15:1-4

Our 21st century global communication system offers both a blessing and a curse. Social media posts can bless countless readers with the truth of God's Word, a note of encouragement, or a challenge to live your best life with God's strength. Social media posts also have the power to promote hatred, distrust, and

Unit 1: Holy Living

Think About It

Jesus made the important connection between the condition of our heart and the way we speak and live in Mark 7:20-23: "He went on: 'What comes out of a person is what defiles them. For it is from within, out of a person's heart, that evil thoughts come—sexual immorality, theft, murder, adultery, greed, malice, deceit, lewdness, envy, slander, arrogance and folly. All these evils come from inside and defile a person.'"

misinformation that can divide families, communities, and entire nations.

Charitable discourse has lost its value in our world. However, the righteous offer gentle answers which calm volatile situations and turn people away from wrathful responses. Their conversation is filled with godly wisdom and knowledge which brings positive benefits. People feel nourished by their words and enjoy listening to them because what they have to say helps them flourish in life.

We often hear contributors to social media platforms feel empowered to say whatever they want to say, regardless of the damage their words might cause, because they remain anonymous. No one at work, school, or the neighborhood will ever know they are the source of hateful or foolish conversation. Verse 3 reminds us that God hears our every word and keeps records. Someday those words will come back to bless or condemn us.

This passage of Scripture ends with the reminder that our tongue welds incredible power to bring results, either good or bad. A tongue that offers soothing or healing words promotes abundant life. A tongue filled with dishonest words crushes listeners' spirits. These words have the power to wound deeply. Believers must always remember that our every conversation can promote or hinder God's name and mission in our world. We must seek to speak in ways that honor God. God can use such conversations to further His work. We can join His efforts of evangelism and discipleship as we honor Him with Christlike dialogue.

REFLECT Do the words you speak build up or tear down?

FRANK MOORE

July

2

CHRISTLIKE SPIRITUAL DISCIPLINES

*Christlike disciples discipline themselves
in order to grow in their faith.*

THE WORD

1 CORINTHIANS 9:24-27

Do you not know that in a race all the runners run, but only one gets the prize? Run in such a way as to get the prize. ²⁵Everyone who competes in the games goes into strict training. They do it to get a crown that will not last, but we do it to get a crown that will last forever. ²⁶Therefore I do not run like someone running aimlessly; I do not fight like a boxer beating the air. ²⁷No, I strike a blow to my body and make it my slave so that after I have preached to others, I myself will not be disqualified for the prize.

LAMENTATIONS 3:21-29

²¹Yet this I call to mind and therefore I have hope:

²²Because of the Lord's great love we are not consumed, for his compassions never fail.

²³They are new every morning; great is your faithfulness.

²⁴I say to myself, "The Lord is my portion; therefore I will wait for him."

KEY VERSE

²⁵ The Lord is good to those whose hope is in him, to the one who seeks him;

²⁶it is good to wait quietly for the salvation of the Lord.

²⁷It is good for a man to bear the yoke while he is young.

²⁸ Let him sit alone in silence, for the Lord has laid it on him.

²⁹Let him bury his face in the dust—there may yet be hope.

1 PETER 4:8-11

⁸Above all, love each other deeply, because love covers over a multitude of sins. ⁹Offer hospitality to one another without grumbling. ¹⁰Each of you should use whatever gift you have received to serve others, as faithful stewards of God's grace in its various forms. ¹¹If

anyone speaks, they should do so as one who speaks the very words of God. If anyone serves, they should do so with the strength God provides, so that in all things God may be praised through Jesus Christ. To him be the glory and the power for ever and ever. Amen.

ENGAGE THE WORD

SIMPLICITY

1 Corinthians 9:24-27

Corinthian Christians immediately identified with Paul's reference to racing. Being a famous sporting event in Corinth, everyone knew the price athletes paid in order to participate in this race.

Paul quickly shifts the attention of his readers from the Corinthian athletic event to the "race" set before every believer in Christ Jesus. Paul encourages his readers, and us, to commit to strict training on a regular basis, running in the race God has signed us up for, and focusing attention on the finish line in order to stay on task until the race is won. Paul reminds us that, like athletes in training, we must deny ourselves everything that hinders our participation in the race and master all of the skills, abilities, and practices that insure our final success.

Paul then compares the treasured prize the best athlete and the Christian believer receive at the finish line. One receives a horticultural garland that wilts with time; the other receives a prize that lasts through all eternity as we live and worship in the unhindered presence of God. Successful runners and faithful Christians chose a life of simplicity. No extra baggage, no divided attention, and no lazy days. A trained mind and body locks eyes on the finish line with a laser focus and refuses to let anything get in the way.

SOLITUDE AND SUBMISSION

Lamentations 3:21-29

The call to solitude and submission in today's Scripture begins with an important reminder: we have an incredible hope in the midst of life's trying circumstances because we serve a God who loves us indescribably, has compassion on us unfailingly, and remains faithful to us daily. The context of this famous declaration of God's love, compassion, and faithfulness might surprise you. You could think the author is on top of the world with everything going right. Not so; quite the opposite. Chapter 3 begins by describing life at its lowest and most desperate point. The word "yet" that introduces verse 21 indicates that the author has chosen to focus attention on God's love, compassion, and faithfulness in the midst of trying circumstances.

"The Lord is my portion" (v. 24) sets the background for the spiritual disciplines of solitude and submission. Most of us live in societies that urge us to jump into action when we find the circumstances of life overwhelming us. We may even hear an inner voice calling us to get up and do something. Christian disciples must resist that urge. If the Lord is truly our portion, the most spiritual thing we can do is "wait for him" (v. 24). Old Testament priests owned no land. God gave them something better than land; He gave them a special sense of His presence as they ministered for Him. Their ministry assignment often required them to wait silently before the Lord.

We often think of waiting as a negative exercise or a sign of defeated resignation. This passage of Scripture reminds us that solitude puts us in the presence of God and submission requires us to wait with expectancy, hope, confidence, and an active faith that God has been working, is now working, and will continue to work in our situation. We can count on God. Why? He is good (v. 25), waiting is good (v. 26), and, as strange as it may sound, suffering can serve a good purpose if we submit to the spiritual discipline that grows us in God's grace (v. 27). Disciples who wait on the Lord in solitude and submission display humility and patience as they place all of their hope and trust in God, confident of His certain deliverance.

SERVICE

1 Peter 4:8-11

No biblical discussion of outward spiritual disci-

Unit 1: Holy Living

Think About It

An individual can exercise discipline and develop virtuous habits through human effort. However, only the power of the Holy Spirit at work in the heart and life of a committed believer can make a person more Christlike.

plines is complete without focusing attention on service. Peter declares that all Christian service flows from love for others. This love must come from the depth of our being. Not simply an emotion, this love calls us to action. Our love for others embraces them in a way that overlooks any sin or wrongdoing they may have committed against us.

We offer our hospitality to benefit others with a cheerful heart, not grumbling under our breath about any hardship it places on us. Early Christians highly valued opening their homes to fellow believers and others in need for a meal and fellowship time. They offer a good example for us today.

Peter emphasized three key principles for believers to minister in service to one another. First, God gives at least one spiritual gift to every believer. This gift is not natural talent or abilities. Rather, it is a God-given endowment. Second, God gives us spiritual gifts for the express purpose of serving others rather than calling attention to our abilities or feeding personal ego. We must faithfully steward God's grace at work in our lives for ministry to others. Third, God distributes a variety of gifts to believers so that all of the needs of communities of faith will be met. Everyone participates in God's plan for His church as we exercise the gift He bestows upon us.

Peter offers a fitting conclusion to this discussion of outward spiritual gifts. That is, in everything we do as believers, "God may be praised through Jesus Christ" (v. 11).

REFLECT In what ways can you incorporate the spiritual disciplines of service, simplicity, submission, and solitude into your life?

FRANK MOORE

July

9

IS GOD A RACIST?

God sets people apart for His kingdom purposes.

THE WORD

DEUTERONOMY 7:1-11

When the LORD your God brings you into the land you are entering to possess and drives out before you many nations—the Hittites, Girgashites, Amorites, Canaanites, Perizzites, Hivites and Jebusites, seven nations larger and stronger than you— ²and when the LORD your God has delivered them over to you and you have defeated them, then you must destroy them totally. Make no treaty with them, and show them no mercy. ³Do not intermarry with them. Do not give your daughters to their sons or take their daughters for your sons, ⁴for they will turn your children away from following me to serve other gods, and the LORD's anger will burn against you and will quickly destroy you. ⁵This is what you are to do to them: Break down their altars, smash their sacred stones, cut down their Asherah poles and burn their idols in the fire. ⁶For you are a people holy to the LORD your God. The LORD your God has chosen you out of all the peoples on the face of the earth to be his people, his treasured possession.

⁷The LORD did not set his affection on you and choose you because you were more numerous than other peoples, for you were the fewest of all peoples. ⁸But it was because the LORD loved you and kept the oath he swore to your ancestors that he brought you out with a mighty hand and redeemed you from the land of slavery, from the power of Pharaoh king of Egypt. ⁹Know therefore that the LORD your God is God; he is the faithful God, keeping his covenant of love to a thousand generations of those who love him and keep his commandments. ¹⁰But those who hate him he will repay to their face by destruction; he will not be slow to repay to their face those who hate him.

¹¹Therefore, take care to follow the commands, decrees and laws I give you today.

GALATIANS 3:26-29

KEY VERSE

²⁶So in Christ Jesus you are all children of God through faith, ²⁷for all of you who were baptized into Christ have clothed yourselves with Christ. **²⁸There is neither Jew nor Gentile, neither slave nor free, nor is there male and female, for you are all one in Christ Jesus.** ²⁹If you belong to Christ, then you are Abraham's seed, and heirs according to the promise.

ENGAGE THE WORD

DESTROY THEM TOTALLY?

Deuteronomy 7:1-6

If we believe Scripture is one of God's good gifts, we also may be sure God intends Scripture to communicate, not to confuse. But Deuteronomy 7 can seem confusing. The Bible is clear that God loves and desires life for every human (famously, John 3:16), having no favorites (Romans 2:11). However, at first glance God's instructions appear harsh. Utterly destroy? Most translations have rendered the word *haram* (cha-RAHM—"ch" as in "loch") as, "You must utterly destroy them," or something similar (v. 2). However, rather than understanding this as the wiping out of persons, a faithful way to translate the word is: "devote to/consecrate to/reserve for [God's purposes]," without reference to killing. Moses reminded Israel (v. 1) that God would "clear away" the Canaanites. What does that mean in practice?

First, they were not to enter into any treaties (make a covenant) with them. Second, they were to show them no mercy. Here, we should translate this as, "You shall not deal graciously/favorably with them" (i.e., do not interact with them in ways that entice you away from faithfulness to God). Third, Israel was not to intermarry with their Canaanite neighbors (vv. 3-4) so that their children would not serve other gods, but only follow and serve God alone. Lastly, God told them to destroy their objects of worship. God directed Israel to destroy them so the pagan worship of

ISRAEL, THE FEWEST OF ALL THE PEOPLES

their Canaanite neighbors would not entice Israel to forsake the one true God.

The command of God was for Israel to remove anything and anyone from their lives that might endanger their relationship with God. They were to remove whatever might keep them from loving God and living the life He called them to live in the promised land. Therefore, God called the people to "clear away" Canaanite culture and destroy the artifacts of Canaan's pagan "deities." This had nothing to with "racism/racial preference." This had everything to do with Israel serving God wholeheartedly.

Deuteronomy 7:7-11

The idea that bigger is better has been around for most of human history. Moses already had reminded Israel they were not that. The Canaanites comprised "seven peoples [not nation-states] larger and stronger" than Israel (v. 1b). Now he went further; in reality, Israel was "the smallest of all the peoples" (v. 7b). In God's assessments, "bigger" is not "better."

If not for impressive numbers or strength, why did God choose Israel (v. 7)? Because of "the oath [God] swore to your ancestors" (v. 8)—God had promised Abraham a family and this land as their inheritance. Abraham had believed God keeps God's oaths. His family—now grown into a "people" ready to enter the land of promise—was one of the first physical evidences that Abraham had not misplaced his faith. (Paul expanded on this in Galatians 3:29; see below.)

There is also the matter of "reversal." Egypt was the wealthiest, most powerful empire of Moses' day, but God (Yahweh) did not choose Egypt. Rather, God "brought [little Israel] out with a mighty hand and redeemed [them] from the land of slavery, from the power [lit., 'from the hand'] of Pharaoh king of Egypt" (v. 8). God delights in such reversal—bringing low those who are mighty, but arrogant and unrepentant, while exalting the humble and believing poor.

Think About It

An important principle is that we are to interpret unclear or confusing biblical passages in the light of other, clearer, passages—not the other way around.

ONE IN CHRIST JESUS

Galatians 3:26-29

Throughout Galatians 3, Paul developed one of the central tenets of his teaching: through faith in Christ, not only Jews (Israelites), but also Gentiles, are "children of Abraham" (v. 7). The climax of the chapter (v. 29) is the culmination of this point, "If you belong to Christ, then you are Abraham's seed, and heirs according to the promise."

People raised in the church today often do not realize the transformational nature of this (to us) commonplace truism. For Paul the Pharisee (Philippians 3:5), before encountering Jesus, the three contrasting pairs of identities he listed in verse 28 were the three unbridgeable divides between persons and groups. Observant Jews were to have as little contact with Gentiles as possible. Yet, here Paul says, in Christ there is neither Jew nor Greek. For everyone in the first-century Greco-Roman world, the divisions between slaves and free persons, and between males and (most) females, were absolute and unquestionable. But Paul asserted there is "neither slave nor free, nor is there male and female, for you are all one in Christ Jesus" (v. 28). In Christ, no place exists for racism, classism, or sexism. Period.

REFLECT If living out Galatians 3:26-29 is central to being "in Christ Jesus," do you need to change anything in your thoughts, attitudes, or actions toward "others"? If so, how could you do that? (Think and plan as specifically and realistically as you can.)

JOSEPH COLESON is professor emeritus of Old Testament at Nazarene Theological Seminary, author of *Genesis 1-11* in the *New Beacon Bible Commentary,* and co-author, with Sarah Derck, of *Song of Solomon* in the NBBC.

July
16

WHY DOES GOD GET ANGRY?

God's anger is directed toward sin, not people.

THE WORD

PSALM 78:17-24

But they continued to sin against him, rebelling in the wilderness against the Most High.

¹⁸They willfully put God to the test by demanding the food they craved.

¹⁹They spoke against God; they said, "Can God really spread a table in the wilderness?

²⁰True, he struck the rock, and water gushed out, streams flowed abundantly, but can he also give us bread? Can he supply meat for his people?"

KEY VERSES

²¹When the Lᴏʀᴅ heard them, he was furious; his fire broke out against Jacob and his wrath rose against Israel,

²²for they did not believe in God or trust in his deliverance.

²³Yet he gave a command to the skies above and opened the doors of the heavens;

²⁴he rained down manna for the people to eat, he gave them the grain of heaven.

ROMANS 1:18-25

¹⁸The wrath of God is being revealed from heaven against all the godlessness and wickedness of people, who suppress the truth by their wickedness, ¹⁹since what may be known about God is plain to them, because God has made it plain to them. ²⁰For since the creation of the world God's invisible qualities—his eternal power and divine nature—have been clearly seen, being understood from what has been made, so that people are without excuse.

²¹For although they knew God, they neither glorified him as God nor gave thanks to him, but their thinking became futile and their

Unit 2: Hard Sayings of the Old Testament

foolish hearts were darkened. [22]Although they claimed to be wise, they became fools [23]and exchanged the glory of the immortal God for images made to look like a mortal human being and birds and animals and reptiles.

[24]Therefore God gave them over in the sinful desires of their hearts to sexual impurity for the degrading of their bodies with one another. [25]They exchanged the truth about God for a lie, and worshiped and served created things rather than the Creator—who is forever praised. Amen.

ENGAGE THE WORD

HUMANKIND'S INSOLENT SKEPTICISM

Psalm 78:17-20

Psalm 78:1-16 is the immediate context of 78:17-20; it emphasizes God's miraculous actions (v. 12) in freeing Israel from Egyptian bondage, but also touches on their faithlessness—Israel "forgot" (v. 11). In our section, forgetting progressed into ungrateful skepticism and brazen insolence. The psalmist summarized both the aggressive nature and the sarcastic tone of Israel's transgression: "Can God really spread a table . . .?" (v. 19); "True, he struck the rock . . ., but can he also give us bread?" (v. 20). Exodus 16:1 puts the beginnings of this faithless response less than two months after Moses led Israel out of Egypt. The psalmist highlights the people's short memory and lack of faith.

GOD'S ANGER

Psalm 78:21-24

It is telling that our Psalm passage contains only three expressions of "anger," all in verse 21. We see in the first reference that God "was furious"; this is from *'br* (ah-VAHR); used "literally," it means to "overflow," as a stream in flood stage may overflow its banks. Metaphorically, as here, it pictures God's cup of fury (wrath) overflowing, spilling out, to effect judgment on transgressors.

The second expression, "his fire broke out against Jacob," records a result, or display, of God's wrath. The verb is passive, literally, "a fire was kindled." The

GOD'S WRATH

third, "his wrath rose," also is a figurative usage, and probably should be translated here, "anger." This Hebrew noun, "*aph* (also translated as nose)," often is used metaphorically as an expression connoting anger, because of the flaring of the nostrils, and/or the flush of the skin (especially of the nose), that can/does occur when an individual becomes angry. The psalmist's reason for God's anger? "They [Israel] did not believe . . . or trust" (v. 22). Despite God's loving care for them, they chose to doubt rather than place their faith in Him.

Romans 1:18-25

Paul's discussion begins (NIV) with "the wrath of God" (v. 18). In the New Testament, this phrase often functions as a legal, judicial term, denoting the sentence or punishment to come upon offenders. "Wrath" is the punishment felt, experienced, and endured by the guilty party as painful and unwelcome, but also understood as a just sentence for the crime. The wrath of God should be understood not as "an unbridled and normless exercise of vengeance, but an indignant response to sin based upon His holy nature."[1] W.T. Purkiser says it is "the unfailing opposition of God's holy love to all that is evil."[2] We experience God's wrath as a result of sin/disobedience. However, the good news is that those who have been justified by the blood of Jesus are "saved from God's wrath through him" (Romans 5:9).

What people *should* know, Paul said, they really *do* know, but refuse to acknowledge, whether in worshiping God, or even "merely" in gratefulness to God (v. 21). Humans will worship, though; so beyond withholding worship from God, pagan subjects of the first-century Roman Empire worshiped "images [idols] made to look like a mortal human being [Caesar, among others] and birds and animals and reptiles" (v. 23). Paul identified humankind's insolent turning from God to worship other "gods" as the catalyst for God's

Think About It

"Sinners experience the wrath of God as the apparently 'natural' consequence of attempting to live at odds with the reality that the Creator exists and that creatures owe him their gratitude and worship. God's wrath is expressed in his refusal to spare sinners from the consequences of their self-destructive folly" (*New Beacon Bible Commentary: Romans 1-8.* [Kansas City: Beacon Hill Press of Kansas City, 2008], 70).

"wrath" (v. 18).

The initial evidence of God's wrath, Paul said, is that "God gave them over" (v. 24) to what--in the misdirected pagan worship of his day--those estranged from God already had been doing anyway. Given the understanding of "wrath" here in its proper judicial sense, his point is that God's wrath is "pending" against all human rebellion.

We do experience and observe some of the corrosive effects of our sin and rebellion even in this age ("the wrath of God is being revealed," v. 18), but only in their earliest stages. That God ultimately will put an end to human rebellion is a prominent eschatological motif in both the Old and the New Testaments, but the final judicial reckoning ("wrath") is not yet. Paul's warning here is a word of mercy; his first readers and hearers, and all since, have time still to accept God's salvation and reconciliation.

Why does God get angry? Why is God's wrath revealed? Primarily, it is because of our rejection of God's offer of intimate relationship—grieving God and harming ourselves, others, and even all God's good creation. Our disregard for God and the things of God evoke His anger. However, unlike human anger, God's anger is righteous and ethically motivated.[3] God's anger does not express His disdain for us, but communicates His strong dislike for sin. It is not an impulsive outburst of emotion, but a response to human disobedience, motivated by holy love.

1 Richard S. Taylor. *Beacon Dictionary of Theology* (Kansas City: Beacon Hill Press of Kansas City, 1983), 552.
2 Ibid, 552.
3 Ibid, 37.

REFLECT What is your understanding of God's anger/wrath?

JOSEPH COLESON

WHY DOES GOD ALLOW PEOPLE TO SUFFER?

Even when we experience suffering,
Christ's glory can be revealed through us.

THE WORD

AMOS 4:6-12

I gave you empty stomachs in every city and lack of bread in every town, yet you have not returned to me," declares the LORD.

⁷"I also withheld rain from you when the harvest was still three months away. I sent rain on one town, but withheld it from another. One field had rain; another had none and dried up.

⁸People staggered from town to town for water but did not get enough to drink, yet you have not returned to me," declares the LORD.

⁹"Many times I struck your gardens and vineyards, destroying them with blight and mildew. Locusts devoured your fig and olive trees, yet you have not returned to me," declares the LORD.

¹⁰"I sent plagues among you as I did to Egypt. I killed your young men with the sword, along with your captured horses. I filled your nostrils with the stench of your camps, yet you have not returned to me," declares the LORD.

¹¹"I overthrew some of you as I overthrew Sodom and Gomorrah. You were like a burning stick snatched from the fire, yet you have not returned to me," declares the LORD.

¹²"Therefore this is what I will do to you, Israel, and because I will do this to you, Israel, prepare to meet your God."

1 PETER 4:12-19

KEY VERSE

¹²Dear friends, do not be surprised at the fiery ordeal that has come on you to test you, as though something strange were happening to you. **¹³But rejoice inasmuch as you participate in the sufferings of Christ, so that you may be overjoyed when his glory is revealed.** ¹⁴If you are insulted because of the name of Christ, you are blessed, for the Spirit of glory and of God rests on you. ¹⁵If you

suffer, it should not be as a murderer or thief or any other kind of criminal, or even as a meddler. [16]However, if you suffer as a Christian, do not be ashamed, but praise God that you bear that name. [17]For it is time for judgment to begin with God's household; and if it begins with us, what will the outcome be for those who do not obey the gospel of God? [18]And, "If it is hard for the righteous to be saved, what will become of the ungodly and the sinner?"

[19]So then, those who suffer according to God's will should commit themselves to their faithful Creator and continue to do good.

ENGAGE THE WORD

"YET YOU HAVE NOT RETURNED TO ME"

Amos 4:6-12

During the time of Amos, urban royal, temple, and economic elites had turned Israel into a centralized, palace-directed, international-market economy, trading with Tyre and other commercial centers (cf. Ezekiel 27:17). Amos called out these elites for their theft of ancestral inheritances, which reduced land-owning families to poverty, tenancy, and even slavery (e.g., Amos 2:6-7; 5:10-13; 8:4-6).

God did not bring final judgment without warning. The first three calamities of our passage are agricultural (v. 6). The most common reason for crop failures in the ancient Highlands was lack of rain, or rain at the "wrong times" in the succession of agricultural seasons. Wheat and barley provided the greater part of the ordinary daily diet; a drought such as Amos noted here severely curtailed the grain harvest, or caused it to fail altogether. That the springs and wells of some towns went completely dry, forcing people to walk to neighboring towns even for drinking water, also points to the severity of these droughts (vv. 7-8). Garden produce, grapes (with wine and raisins), figs, and olives comprised most of the rest of the average family's diet; when these, too, were destroyed by disease or insect pests, people really became desperate (v. 9).

Eighth-century Israel also undertook military adventures, but God sometimes undermined their success

(v. 10). In some cases, an enemy's destruction of a captured town could be compared with that of Sodom and Gomorrah (v. 11). Through all this obvious and multiplied disaster, agricultural, and military, Israel's response was the same. To be sure his hearers could not miss his point, Amos repeated five times the refrain, "Yet you have not returned to me" (vv. 6, 8, 9, 10, 11). Amos invoked the memory of the plagues of Egypt in his attempt to awaken Jeroboam II's Israel (v. 10).

A large percentage of "pains" we experience are (and always have been) the result of our own or others' sin, ignorance, sloth, carelessness, and so on, and should not be attributed to God. Despite the given circumstances we are facing, God can, and does, use them to "shout" to us in the attempt to draw us (back) to God's own self—to redeem and restore us.

IF YOU SUFFER AS A CHRISTIAN

1 Peter 4:12-19

Peter wrote to Christians "scattered throughout" several Roman provinces (1 Peter 1:1) Many Christians were suffering snubs, harassment, and discrimination simply for being Christian. Some had been imprisoned, and at least a few had been martyred. In virtually all moral and ethical systems, not the innocent, but the wicked, are "supposed" to experience suffering. Many were asking: "Why us? What are we to do?"

Much of 1 Peter addresses these questions, both directly and indirectly. An important part of Peter's answer is that Christ suffered, so we should not expect to escape suffering along with Him. Rather, we should endure and take joy in our suffering, because it shows we belong to Him.

Another aspect of Peter's encouragement in our passage is based on the recognition that, in this world awash with the negative consequences of human rebellion against our Creator/Sustainer, every human (and much of the created order) suffers; ultimately, suffering is inescapable. "As though something strange were happening to you" (v. 12) acknowledges trials and suffering are a present reality for believers.

That being so, Peter counsels his readers and hearers, "Then do not let any [among] you suffer as a murderer, or as a thief, or as an evildoer, or [even] as a meddler [in the affairs of others]"[†] (v. 15). All such moral/ethical transgressions increase and/or intensify the myriad kinds of suffering and tend toward the breakdown of creational order. Since everyone born of woman will suffer to a greater or lesser degree—and especially with eternity in view—it is better by far to suffer as a Christian: "Do not be ashamed, but praise God that you bear that name" (v. 16).

Moreover, suffering with Christ will have its ultimate reward. Peter assures us a time is coming "when [Christ's] glory is revealed" (v. 13), and that the "spirit of glory . . . is resting on you" (v. 14). Glory is not only the praise and adulation that comes from doing well something difficult, or even dangerous. In his sermon, "The Weight of Glory," C.S. Lewis rightly defined glory as being and/or doing what someone or something is "supposed" to—was designed or sent to be or do. Sent by the Father, Jesus "has destroyed death" (2 Timothy 1:10). That is His glory—His generosity is that as we now share in His suffering, He will give us also to share in His glory (Romans 8:17).

REFLECT Suffering can be complicated, and so can its cause(s). How can you learn to discern the reason(s) for your suffering? Why can discernment be important, and how can it be helpful?

JOSEPH COLESON

July

30

DOES GOD NOT FORGIVE SOME PEOPLE?

God forgives the truly repentant.

THE WORD

1 SAMUEL 15:24-35

Then Saul said to Samuel, "I have sinned. I violated the LORD's command and your instructions. I was afraid of the men and so I gave in to them. ²⁵Now I beg you, forgive my sin and come back with me, so that I may worship the LORD."

²⁶But Samuel said to him, "I will not go back with you. You have rejected the word of the LORD, and the LORD has rejected you as king over Israel!"

²⁷As Samuel turned to leave, Saul caught hold of the hem of his robe, and it tore. ²⁸Samuel said to him, "The LORD has torn the kingdom of Israel from you today and has given it to one of your neighbors—to one better than you. ²⁹He who is the Glory of Israel does not lie or change his mind; for he is not a human being, that he should change his mind."

³⁰Saul replied, "I have sinned. But please honor me before the elders of my people and before Israel; come back with me, so that I may worship the LORD your God." ³¹So Samuel went back with Saul, and Saul worshiped the LORD.

³²Then Samuel said, "Bring me Agag king of the Amalekites."

Agag came to him in chains. And he thought, "Surely the bitterness of death is past."

³³But Samuel said, "As your sword has made women childless, so will your mother be childless among women."

And Samuel put Agag to death before the LORD at Gilgal.

³⁴Then Samuel left for Ramah, but Saul went up to his home in Gibeah of Saul. ³⁵Until the day Samuel died, he did not go to see Saul again, though Samuel mourned for him. And the LORD regretted that he had made Saul king over Israel.

ACTS 13:38-39

³⁸"Therefore, my friends, I want you to know that through Jesus the forgiveness of sins is proclaimed to you. ³⁹Through him everyone who believes is set free from every sin, a justification you were not able to obtain under the law of Moses.

1 JOHN 1:8-9

KEY VERSE

⁸If we claim to be without sin, we deceive ourselves and the truth is not in us. **⁹If we confess our sins, he is faithful and just and will forgive us our sins and purify us from all unrighteousness.**

ENGAGE THE WORD

THE ALL-IMPORTANT PRONOUN

1 Samuel 15:24-35

First Samuel 15 begins with Saul's campaign against Amalek. God had given Saul a command (v. 3) and Saul did that, up to a point. He did not execute Amalek's King Agag for what today we would call war crimes. He also spared the best livestock, trying to shift blame for that to "the people" (vv. 20-21). God now "rejected" Saul (v. 23).

Saul asked for God's forgiveness (vv. 24-25). Samuel repeated God's rejection (v. 26) and as Samuel turned away, Saul tore his robe. Samuel proclaimed that (others were within hearing) as a sign that God had "torn the kingdom" from Saul (vv. 27-28). Saul repeated his request that Samuel "honor" him by going with him to sacrifice to God—here, "honor" means, most importantly, "not shame" him publicly by refusing to go with him. This time, Samuel complied with Saul's request (vv. 30-31), but the scene ends with Samuel's execution of Agag (vv. 32-33).

This scene requires a closer look in light of today's two New Testament selections and the many other indications of God's justice and mercy throughout Scripture. This event does not define what some Christians today would refer to as Saul's "personal relationship with God." God's judgment of Saul's failure with Agag and the best of Amalek's spoils of war reflect his performance as king, not his "state of grace" (though we shall see that the two are related). God's rejection of Saul as Israel's king is not evidence for, let alone proof

BELIEF, CONFESSION, FORGIVENESS

of, God's "rejection" of any human as one whom God will or will not forgive, personally.

Entreating Samuel, Saul said, "Come back with me, that I may worship *your* God" (emphasis added). Not "*my* God," but "*your* God!" (v. 30). Somewhere along the way Saul rejected the God of Israel as his own God. God rejected Saul as the dynastic king of Israel, but God did not reject Saul as one who could believe in and worship God. Whether Saul repented and found God's forgiveness as his life ended (31:4-5) we cannot know. Relying on the two New Testament passages we now turn to, we can be confident that, if Saul repented, God forgave and accepted him even in that final hour.

Acts 13:38-39

Acts 13:38-39 essentially culminates Paul's introduction of Jesus in his sermon to Jews and God-fearing Gentiles in the synagogue of Antioch in Pisidia, in south-central Asia Minor (in today's Turkey).

Most in the synagogue probably were hearing for the first time anything detailed or significant about Jesus. Paul's closing statement, "Through him everyone who believes is set free from every sin" (v. 39), would have sounded strange and fantastical to many. Everyone who believes what? Paul's answer to that is in verse 30, a kind of "first climax" to his sermon, "God raised him from the dead." To Paul's audience, such a claim was impossible believe—as it would be to most of us if we heard it now for the first time. Yet Paul made that claim, and in the following days in Antioch, many who heard him began to believe it.

Contrary to popular belief, the ancients were not naively credulous. They needed proof, just as we do. Many have posited explanations for Jesus' tomb being empty that third morning. Some of the most popular: Jesus did not really die, but "swooned" and was resuscitated after being brought down from the cross; Jesus' followers stole His body; the temple authori-

Think About It

John's reference to those who "claimed" not to have sinned is a direct refutation of those (called Gnostics) who denied their immoral actions were sinful. The Gnostics presented the early church with one of its most dangerous challenges. The word "sin" is a key concept in 1 John, mentioned 27 times.

CONFESSION

ties moved His body; the women, and later the men, came to the wrong tomb by mistake. All these (and all others) have been proven impossible. We are left with the testimony of more than 500 witnesses (1 Corinthians 15:6)—not one of whom ever recanted, though many died for their refusal to say they had lied. Most reasonable people consider such evidence credible, even compelling; many come to believe in Jesus and the forgiveness He made available. Some of Paul's audience in Pisidian Antioch were among those, as were John's readers and hearers.

Jesus' death, burial, and resurrection—His victory over sin and death—is proof that God can and does forgive us our rebellion and the sins we have committed. That was Jesus' "mission" in coming as a human to this earth. The good news is that "everyone" that believes in Jesus is set free from sin (Acts 10:43).

1 John 1:8-9

If we believe God can and does forgive us, confession of sin reasonably follows. Why "claim to be without sin" (1:8) when we know that to be untrue and God's forgiveness renders sin powerless? Why would we not confess our rebellion and sins when, upon our confession, God "is faithful and just and will forgive . . . and purify us" (v. 9)?

The good news of the gospel is that no matter what a person has done or how deep in sin a person has sunk, God's forgiveness is available to all who come to Him in faith (John 3:16).

REFLECT Take time to reflect on the reality of God's forgiveness.

JOSEPH COLESON

FIGHTING FOR THE FAITH

The church needs leadership that will set a godly example and constantly fight for the faith of fellow believers.

THE WORD

TITUS 1:1-16

Paul, a servant of God and an apostle of Jesus Christ to further the faith of God's elect and their knowledge of the truth that leads to godliness—²in the hope of eternal life, which God, who does not lie, promised before the beginning of time, ³and which now at his appointed season he has brought to light through the preaching entrusted to me by the command of God our Savior,

⁴To Titus, my true son in our common faith:

Grace and peace from God the Father and Christ Jesus our Savior.

⁵The reason I left you in Crete was that you might put in order what was left unfinished and appoint elders in every town, as I directed you. ⁶An elder must be blameless, faithful to his wife, a man whose children believe and are not open to the charge of being wild and disobedient. ⁷Since an overseer manages God's household, he must be blameless—not overbearing, not quick-tempered, not given to drunkenness, not violent, not pursuing dishonest gain. **⁸Rather, he must be hospitable, one who loves what is good, who is self-controlled, upright, holy and disciplined.** ⁹He must hold firmly to the trustworthy message as it has been taught, so that he can encourage others by sound doctrine and refute those who oppose it.

KEY VERSE

¹⁰For there are many rebellious people, full of meaningless talk and deception, especially those of the circumcision group. ¹¹They must be silenced, because they are disrupting whole households by teaching things they ought not to teach—and that for the sake of dishonest gain. ¹²One of Crete's own prophets has said it: "Cretans are always liars, evil brutes, lazy gluttons." ¹³This saying is true. Therefore

rebuke them sharply, so that they will be sound in the faith ¹⁴and will pay no attention to Jewish myths or to the merely human commands of those who reject the truth. ¹⁵To the pure, all things are pure, but to those who are corrupted and do not believe, nothing is pure. In fact, both their minds and consciences are corrupted. ¹⁶They claim to know God, but by their actions they deny him. They are detestable, disobedient and unfit for doing anything good.

ENGAGE THE WORD

THE STANDARDS FOR CHURCH LEADERSHIP

Titus 1:1-6

The letter to Titus is instructions for a very crude and ignorant culture on Crete. He commissioned Titus to straighten out the mess by appointing elders. Leaders with integrity, self-control, and biblical knowledge were needed to confront and straighten out the mess caused by the "rebellious," those looking for "dishonest gain," and "lazy gluttons" with no self-control.

The standards for church leadership in Titus are high, but we should not think that these expectations are only for leaders. The standards we find here are for all believers, but especially for those in leadership who must lead by example.

The leader must be "blameless." That is a high standard! We tend to think of this word as being faultless or perfect, but that is not the meaning in this context. The word has to do with one's personal integrity. This integrity extends to the leaders' personal lives in marital faithfulness and in living a life of integrity before their children. While children need to make their own decisions about following Christ, the integrity of their parents as Christian leaders goes a long way in helping them to know what real Christians are like. Integrity in marriage is still difficult to maintain today. However, it is a necessary part of our Christian testimony and integrity. Marriage is a sacred covenant and takes constant cultivation and communication to keep it strong. When we say we love our spouse, our actions must also show that love.

Paul's standard of leadership that includes the children is a more tricky application. The first century was a group-centered culture in which the good of the group (family) was more important than the desires of the individual within that group. Today, children are encouraged to be their own person and see it as a natural process of maturation. In Paul's day, all children were socialized not to shame their families. Only the most defiant and rebellious children would go against their parents' wishes.

While it is important that we experience, know, and decide for ourselves what we believe and value as we grow into adulthood, that is not the same as rebellion. The rebellion that Paul did not want to see in the children of leadership was that which parents who lacked integrity in their lives caused. Children see everything and when we preach one thing and do another in the privacy of our own homes, our integrity crumples in front of our children.

BEING BLAMELESS

Titus 1:7-9

Paul continues in Titus 1:7 using the term "blameless," but this time focusing on self-control. Leaders will encounter frustrations, but how they deal with them reveals the extent to which they have self-control. Paul warns against leaders who always want their own way for their own benefit. In other words, they are "me" focused, rather than "others" focused. This "me" focus can lead to a quick-temper which lashes out when one's personal goals are not met and may even result in verbal or physical violence. When leaders focus on their own needs, they can be tempted to make decisions that will benefit only themselves at the expense of their people. This "dishonest gain" can be more than just money. Fame and status are powerful motivations when one loses self-control.

In Titus 1:8-9, Paul turns to the more positive qualifications of being "hospitable," loving what is good, "self-controlled, upright, holy and disciplined."

Think About It

Two essential qualities of the Christian leader: 1) Their lives reflect their faith as they live according to God's commandments. 2) The ability to teach sound doctrine and in the process repudiate bad teaching.

REBUKE THE REBELLIOUS

In Paul's day, being hospitable was one of the most important virtues. A person who was not hospitable was not a good citizen. Today, being hospitable refers to those who like to have people over to their homes. However, this virtue is more encompassing. It is a posture of acceptance of all kinds of people and an "other" focused perspective. Upright and holy define the good. This indicates that the "good" leaders love has a moral quality defined by God and His Scriptures.

Titus 1:10-16

In Titus 1:10-16, Paul commands Titus, through the leaders he puts in place, to rebuke those who are rebelling against the gospel. These people are disrupting whole households, denying the gospel by their actions and are "detestable, disobedient, and unfit for doing anything good" (v. 16). The first century was an honor/shame culture, which means that the way people learned right from wrong was to shame the disobedient and honor those doing the right thing. Paul was asking Titus to shame those "of the circumcision" who were proclaiming a false gospel, so that people would know that what they were preaching was wrong.

While we do need to teach people what is right and wrong, we can do that by intentional discipleship. In the end, truth will win out. It may take some time and stress, but we continue doing what God has called us to do as leaders: nurturing and protecting God's people from those who would lead them astray.

REFLECT In what way does the behavior of Christians effect the willingness of non-believers to accept the Christian gospel?

C. JEANNE ORJALA SERRÃO is professor of Bible and Intercultural-Studies at Mount Vernon Nazarene University. She is an ordained elder and author of several books, including the commentary on *James* for the *New Beacon Bible Commentary* series.

TEACHING THE FAITH

*Believers need to teach other believers
how Christians live.*

THE WORD

**TITUS
2:1-15**

You, however, must teach what is appropriate to sound doctrine. ²Teach the older men to be temperate, worthy of respect, self-controlled, and sound in faith, in love and in endurance.

³Likewise, teach the older women to be reverent in the way they live, not to be slanderers or addicted to much wine, but to teach what is good. ⁴Then they can urge the younger women to love their husbands and children, ⁵to be self-controlled and pure, to be busy at home, to be kind, and to be subject to their husbands, so that no one will malign the word of God.

⁶Similarly, encourage the young men to be self-controlled. ⁷In everything set them an example by doing what is good. In your teaching show integrity, seriousness ⁸and soundness of speech that cannot be condemned, so that those who oppose you may be ashamed because they have nothing bad to say about us.

⁹Teach slaves to be subject to their masters in everything, to try to please them, not to talk back to them, ¹⁰and not to steal from them, but to show that they can be fully trusted, so that in every way they will make the teaching about God our Savior attractive.

¹¹For the grace of God has appeared that offers salvation to all people. ¹²It teaches us to say "No" to ungodliness and worldly passions, and to live self-controlled, upright and godly lives in this present age, ¹³while we wait for the blessed hope—the appearing of the glory of our great God and Savior, Jesus Christ, ¹⁴who gave himself for us to redeem us from all wickedness and to purify for himself a people that are his very own, eager to do what is good.

KEY VERSE   ¹⁵**These, then, are the things you should teach. Encourage and rebuke with all authority. Do not let anyone despise you.**

ENGAGE THE WORD

TEACH WHAT IS GOOD

Titus 2:1-3

Paul begins with those who hold the most responsibility for the conduct of their society, older men and women. Everyone looked to these people for guidance and example. Today, those of us who are older should know better how to live a good life, but I am not sure that we are the only ones people look to for guidance and example. Therefore, we need to expand the people to whom these directions are given to include those who are the influencers in our church communities. Certainly, these would include both lay and professional leaders.

GOOD TEACHERS

Titus 2:4-8

Some interpreters would like to take verses 1-6 more literally, limiting the instructions to just those Paul addresses, older men and women, and younger men and women. However, this interpretation does not consider the first century culture. Certainly, older Christian men and women should be good Christian examples, but this ignores their ancient roles and gives a pass to young influencers in our congregations. If one is to take the position of teacher or influencer, one must also be an example of self-control and kindness.

In this context, older women were to seek to be good teachers so they could mentor the younger women. Paul gives seven qualities that marked the godly wife of that time. (What about young women who are not married? In Paul's time, it was extremely rare for women above the age of 20 to be unmarried, unless they were widows.) Certainly young women who are wives and mothers should love their husbands and children (see **Did You Know?**). The love, family commitment, and purity of these young women, developed through self-control and training, ought to stand out. The result would be a testimony to the power of the Word of God.

Paul also gives direction to young men. Titus was to be a model to them of what is good and his teaching should demonstrate integrity, seriousness, and sound speech. His example should be such that those who oppose him would not have anything negative to say about him. The result of his modeling would be a visible and effective witness for Christ.

Paul's principle here is that Christians should be good citizens, meeting at least the minimum expectations of their culture for a good person.

BE TRUSTWORTHY

Titus 2:9-10

The contextual nature of this passage becomes even more obvious when Paul addresses what to teach slaves. Again, what Paul said were the expected societal roles for slaves, "subject to their masters, to try to please them, not to talk back to them, and not to steal from them" (vv. 9-10). Today, even the idea of a slave is abhorrent to us. If we find people in slavery, whether child labor or sex trafficking, we would want them to escape their slavery, not remain in it. In fact, advocating for them to stay in their slavery and be submissive to their masters would say to our world that we are not good people!

So what can we do with these two verses? Shall we completely ignore them or can we take something from them? Some would suggest that our conduct as employees could be related to this passage. Certainly, meeting the standard of being a good employee is one way of showing those who need Christ that Christians are good people. Perhaps the injunctions not to steal from our employers and to show them that we can be completely trusted are appropriate. However, the main idea here is to be considered good citizens by our neighbors so that we will "make the teaching about God our Savior attractive" (2:10).

46

Did You Know?

What does Paul mean by saying women should be "busy at home" and "submissive to their husbands" (v. 5)? He was not saying women should not do things outside the home or be servants of their husbands. Paul was saying that, as mothers, they were not to neglect their family responsibilities, which included a mutual respect between husband and wife that "creates space for love to be given and received" (*New Beacon Bible Commentary: 1 & 2 Timothy/Titus* [Kansas City: Beacon Hill Press of Kansas City, 2016], 422.)

TEACH WITH AUTHORITY

GOD'S GRACE

Titus 2:11-13

God's grace offers salvation that teaches us "to say 'No' to ungodliness and worldly passions, and to live self-controlled, upright and godly lives in this present age, while we wait for the blessed hope—the appearing of the glory of our great God and Savior, Jesus Christ." The key words in this section are similar to what we have already heard in chapter 1.

Let us break down what Paul is saying here. First, God's grace saves us and empowers us to live godly lives. Paul is not listing what we need to be doing within our own power. Our godly actions are a result of salvation. Secondly, salvation empowers us not just to know what not to do, but also to know what to do. We can say no to what goes against God's will for His people and we can say yes to what pleases God. Paul characterizes the issues around self-control. Those without self-control are ungodly. Those with self-control are godly. Salvation empowers us to have self-control and God expects us to use it. In our current context, the principle is that God empowers us and expects us to do what is right, not just what feels right. This is how we are to live while we wait for Jesus' return.

Titus 2:14-15

Paul said in conclusion (vv. 14-15), Jesus Christ died to redeem and purify us, making us His own, so that we are "eager to do what is good." We are to teach all these things with the authority that God gives us, making sure to encourage those doing the right things and correcting those who are getting it wrong.

REFLECT What do you think about a person's actions revealing what they really believe? Does this ring true in your experience?

C. JEANNE ORJALA SERRÃO

August

20

FOCUSING ON THE FAITH

Christians are called to live holy lives in a contentious world.

THE WORD

TITUS 3:1-11

Remind the people to be subject to rulers and authorities, to be obedient, to be ready to do whatever is good, ²to slander no one, to be peaceable and considerate, and always to be gentle toward everyone.

³At one time we too were foolish, disobedient, deceived and enslaved by all kinds of passions and pleasures. We lived in malice and envy, being hated and hating one another. ⁴But when the kindness and love of God our Savior appeared, ⁵he saved us, not because of righteous things we had done, but because of his mercy. He saved us through the washing of rebirth and renewal by the Holy Spirit, ⁶whom he poured out on us generously through Jesus Christ our Savior, ⁷so that, having been justified by his grace, we might become heirs having the hope of eternal life. ⁸This is a trustworthy saying. And I want you to stress these things, so that those who have trusted in God may be careful to devote themselves to doing what is good. These things are excellent and profitable for everyone.

KEY VERSE **⁹But avoid foolish controversies and genealogies and arguments and quarrels about the law, because these are unprofitable and useless.** ¹⁰Warn a divisive person once, and then warn them a second time. After that, have nothing to do with them. ¹¹You may be sure that such people are warped and sinful; they are self-condemned.

ENGAGE THE WORD

DOING GOOD

Titus 3:1-2

The two verses that begin chapter 3 continue the same theme of doing "good" as a result of salvation. Paul broadens his audience here to include all the people. Most, or perhaps even all, of those Paul addresses are a conquered people with Rome occupying their island. Paul encourages them to be obedient and subject to all the authorities, signaling to anyone reading his letter that he is not trying to overthrow the Roman Empire. This, along with the instructions not to slander anyone and to be peaceful, considerate, and gentle toward everyone (v. 2), continues the theme of being good citizens from chapter 2.

These instructions concern two different groups that would have control over the lives of the Christians in Crete. One group is the Roman Empire and its delegated authorities and the other group is the Cretan society in which they live. Both of these could severely affect the lives of these Christians and the communication of the message of salvation. Paul cares deeply about both.

YOU ONCE WERE . . . BUT NOW

Titus 3:3-5a

Paul identifies with the Cretan people in verse 3, describing himself and his co-workers, before their salvation, in extremely negative terms. We read in Titus 1:12, "One of Crete's own prophets has said it: 'Cretans are always liars, evil brutes, lazy gluttons.'" Cretans had a very bad reputation in the first century and Paul does nothing to dispel this reputation. Instead, he identifies with them.

Paul, the one who advanced beyond most of his peers in his study of the Torah (Galatians 1:14), a Hebrew of the Hebrews (Philippians 3:5), identifies with a society that would make even other pagan societies cringe! Paul's humbleness shines through. It comes from a heart convinced that God can save and transform anyone.

BECAUSE OF HIS MERCY

Paul contrasts dramatically the nastiness of the pre-conversion life with the "kindness and love of God our Savior" (v. 4). God saved them, not because of how good they were, but because of His mercy. There is no way people can, in their own strength, be good enough to earn salvation. Therefore, it does not matter whether one has a trashed reputation or whether one is considered "the good girl/boy," we are all saved and transformed because of the mercy of God.

Titus 3:5b-8

We read in verse 8, "This is a trustworthy saying," indicating that what came before this was a creed or confession of faith that was widely known in the early Christian world. So let us break down this statement of faith and see what it includes.

God saved us by "the washing of rebirth." We hear echoes of Jesus' teaching in John 3, when questioned by Nicodemus. We are born anew, in a spiritual sense, and become a part of God's family. Rebirth is also a washing, or cleansing, from the impurity of our former lives. This describes the crisis nature of salvation. Just as there is a moment of natural birth, so there is a moment of spiritual birth. We find the process aspect of salvation in the "renewal by the Holy Spirit." Salvation is initiated by God's mercy, happens in a moment of spiritual rebirth, but continues in a process of renewal by the Holy Spirit. While Paul emphasizes here God's actions in salvation, he is not denying the role of the human in cooperating with God's grace. However, because of the contrast between the nastiness of the Cretan reputation and what a Christian should look like, Paul makes sure they understand that it is the all-powerful God that cleanses, transforms, and renews the individual. The effectiveness of the process of transformation has nothing to do with how sinful the person was. God has the power to transform anyone.

The Holy Spirit is poured out on God's people through Jesus Christ (v. 6). This reminds us of the

Think About It
In our daily interactions with each other in the church and in our grace-filled outreach to those beyond the church, we bear witness to the gospel, the good news!

DISCIPLING AND GUIDING

post-resurrection story in John 20:22 when Jesus appears to His frightened disciples who were behind locked doors. Jesus sends them out into the world, just as the Father sent Him. Then He "breathed on them and he said, 'Receive the Holy Spirit.'" The power of the Holy Spirit in their lives is what transformed these frightened disciples and enabled them to do the work of God on earth. The Holy Spirit empowers and enables transformation to take place so that we can do what is "good" (v. 8).

Titus 3:9-11

Paul could have ended his letter with the good news of transformation, but has one more piece of advice for Titus. He warns him to keep on track with the business of discipling and guiding his congregations there in Crete and not get sidetracked by unnecessary theological arguments. The Judaizers who had pursued Paul all over Asia Minor and Greece were apparently causing problems in Crete as well. Paul has obviously had enough of their salvation by works arguments calling them "unprofitable and useless" (v. 9).

When Satan cannot deceive us, he loves to sidetrack us with all kinds of useless arguments with people who will not listen or change their minds. There is a lesson here for all of us. We need to keep focused on the work before us: nurturing and discipling believers. Paul provides a process for dealing with divisive people. Warn them twice and after that ignore them. According to Paul, they are "warped and sinful," and clearly unrepentant. By their own actions, they have condemned themselves and we do not need to feel guilty about the choices they make.

REFLECT If it is the power of the Holy Spirit in our lives that transforms the individual, what are the possibilities of change in your congregation or community?

C. JEANNE ORJALA SERRÃO

August

27

REFRESHING THE HEART

The gospel has power to transform human relationships and bring about reconciliation.

THE WORD

PHILEMON 1:1-21

Paul, a prisoner of Christ Jesus, and Timothy our brother, to Philemon our dear friend and fellow worker—²also to Apphia our sister and Archippus our fellow soldier—and to the church that meets in your home:

³Grace and peace to you from God our Father and the Lord Jesus Christ.

⁴I always thank my God as I remember you in my prayers, ⁵because I hear about your love for all his holy people and your faith in the Lord Jesus. ⁶I pray that your partnership with us in the faith may be effective in deepening your understanding of every good thing we share for the sake of Christ. **⁷Your love has given me great joy and encouragement, because you, brother, have refreshed the hearts of the Lord's people.**

KEY VERSE

⁸Therefore, although in Christ I could be bold and order you to do what you ought to do, ⁹yet I prefer to appeal to you on the basis of love. It is as none other than Paul—an old man and now also a prisoner of Christ Jesus—¹⁰that I appeal to you for my son Onesimus, who became my son while I was in chains. ¹¹Formerly he was useless to you, but now he has become useful both to you and to me.

¹²I am sending him—who is my very heart—back to you. ¹³I would have liked to keep him with me so that he could take your place in helping me while I am in chains for the gospel. ¹⁴But I did not want to do anything without your consent, so that any favor you do would not seem forced but would be voluntary. ¹⁵Perhaps the reason he was separated from you for a little while was that you might have him back forever—¹⁶no longer as a slave, but better than a slave, as

Unit 3: Titus and Philemon

a dear brother. He is very dear to me but even dearer to you, both as a fellow man and as a brother in the Lord.

[17]So if you consider me a partner, welcome him as you would welcome me. [18]If he has done you any wrong or owes you anything, charge it to me. [19]I, Paul, am writing this with my own hand. I will pay it back—not to mention that you owe me your very self. [20]I do wish, brother, that I may have some benefit from you in the Lord; refresh my heart in Christ. [21]Confident of your obedience, I write to you, knowing that you will do even more than I ask.

ENGAGE THE WORD

Philemon was a wealthy member of the church in Colossae who offered his house for meetings. Paul calls him a fellow-laborer. This indicates that he was a very involved and supportive layperson. Paul himself converted him (v. 19), probably during the several months Paul ministered in the Ephesian area.

IN MY PRAYERS

Philemon 1:1-7

Paul wrote the letter to Philemon using the classic structure of first century Roman letters. He begins with a salutation. Then he states to whom he is writing, Philemon, described as a dear friend and co-worker. Paul also includes Apphia and Archippus whom scholars think were Philemon's wife and son. The typical Christianized peace greeting that Paul often used in his letters follows.

The second section of the classic letter was a thanksgiving and prayer. Here we learn what a wonderful Christian Philemon was. He loved all his fellow Christians in Colossae and had a reputation for a strong faith in Jesus Christ. Philemon has brought "great joy and encouragement" to Paul because he has "refreshed the hearts of the Lord's people" (v. 7). This key word translated "refreshed" is in the perfect passive tense indicating that what Philemon had done in the past was still encouraging or refreshing the saints who heard of his good work.

ONESIMUS
Philemon 1:8-16

In the light of Philemon's reputation above, Paul begins his appeal for Onesimus. Paul, because of his position as an apostle, could command him to take Onesimus back; he prefers to appeal to him based on love. Interestingly, he appeals to Philemon by calling himself "an old man and now also a prisoner of Christ Jesus" (v. 9). From our modern perspective this seems to be an appeal from vulnerability, but the Greek terms used here and understood in a first century context could mean something different.

In Ephesians 3:1, when Paul inserts his name, it is to add authority to what he is saying. He also couples his name with the fact that he is "the prisoner of Jesus Christ for the sake of the Gentiles" (Ephesians 3:1). The Greek word translated here as "old man," is also translated as "elder" in many other places in the New Testament. Paul has his associates appoint elders in the churches as part of the organization for the continuing of the churches after Paul and his associates leave. If we interpret verse 9 in light of other letters of Paul and the meaning of these words in the first century, these 3 terms—*Paul, elder,* and *prisoner*—could suggest Paul's authority and the reason why he could command Philemon to take back Onesimus. However, Paul would rather appeal to Philemon based on love.

Another interpretation question here is what love is Paul talking about? Is it Paul's love for Philemon, Philemon's love for Paul, or the nature of God's love? While the text is open-ended, perhaps interpreting love in the broadest Christian sense fits this context. Paul is asking Philemon to treat Onesimus as a brother in the Lord. This was unthinkable for most Gentiles of this era, however it was possible from Paul's perspective because "God's love has been poured out into our hearts through the Holy Spirit" (Romans 5:5). Clearly, the love of God can change the nature of society's

Unit 3: Titus and Philemon

structure and eventually change the unjust structures themselves.

Philemon 1:17-21

In this last section, Paul urges Philemon to welcome Onesimus back as he would welcome Paul. Paul offers to pay or make restitution for anything Onesimus might owe Philemon. Interestingly, Paul uses his proper name again and mentions that Philemon owes Paul "your very self" (v. 19), again indicating that Paul could command all this and not pay anything because of what he has done for Philemon already. In verse 20, Paul uses the term "refresh" that we encountered in verse 7, but this time asking Philemon to encourage Paul's heart by his willing obedience and by welcoming Onesimus because of the love of God, given to Philemon by the Holy Spirit.

Because Paul knows Philemon and because of Philemon's reputation for doing "good," Paul says he knows he will "do even more than" (v. 21) Paul is asking him. Here the themes of Titus that the Christians of Crete would be known for doing "good" and the refreshing or encouraging of God's people and Paul come together. It is by the power of the love of God, which has been poured out in the lives of Christians like Philemon, that "good" can be done in this world and transform the lives and the unjust structures of society.

> **Think About It**
>
> Although there were different ways and reasons why a person became a slave, most people became slaves due to debt. Today, we hear of people who go through bankruptcy. In Paul's day, those people would have ended up as slaves, working to pay off their debts.

A WARM WELCOME

REFLECT If doing "good" refreshes or encourages God's people, what "good" can we do in our particular communities that will encourage Christians?

C. JEANNE ORJALA SERRÃO

Key Verse Memory

Committing God's Word to memory is an important goal for Christians of every age. To assist you in this worthy objective, we have suggested three key verses for memorization. Select one verse to memorize each month or memorize one verse of your choosing for the quarter.

Key verses for Summer 2023:

Romans 12:2

Galatians 3:28

1 John 1:9

COMING NEXT QUARTER

FALL 2023

Unit 1: Lessons from the Kings of Judah [2 Chronicles]
The kings of Judah were powerful and influential. Some were good and others not so good. We will examine the lessons learned from these leaders.

Unit 2: The Message of Ezekiel
God revealed himself to Ezekiel in many wonderful ways. In this study, we will explore these encounters and discover what they teach us about God.

THE FOUNDRY
PUBLISHING